THE LITTLE BOOK OF **BIG** WISDOM

BY SALLY GLENN

Copyright © 2016

All rights reserved. This book or any portion thereof may not be reproduced or used in any manner whatsoever without the express written permission of the author except for the use of brief quotations in a book review.

Printed in Australia
First Printing, 2016
ISBN: 978-0-9945052-8-6

White Light Publishing House
6 Lincoln Way
Melton West, VIC, Australia 3337
www.whitelightpublishingau.com

Preface

This is a book about life. About everyday events that happen to us all, and with which some people struggle to cope, sometimes resulting in emotional distress and breakdowns. Sometimes, we simply overthink life and it is this simple.

The purpose of this book is to offer the reader some alternate perspectives. It is done so in a raw, honest and unfiltered manner. You may find the language in this book is not always delivered lightly or lovingly, and this is deliberate. Sometimes we need guidance delivered with cold hard truth.

Nothing is ever fixed, although it may sometimes seem so. And while it may not be apparent at the time, there is always a bigger picture in play. Nothing is random. There are no accidents. But there is more than one possibility to any situation, and you are always able to alter your experience of life. You do have the power to shift things.

Hopefully this book will give you some insight and trigger within you an intuitive knowing and a sense of peace. At the very least, it will provide some guidance and direction.

You may choose to read this book in sequence, or open to random pages for the message you most need at the time. It is perhaps best read slowly and with consideration, no more than one page per day.

It is my sincerest wish that you find peace, acceptance and possibility in your life.

THE LITTLE BOOK OF **BIG** WISDOM

Remember that you are a *sovereign being*. You have the freedom to choose your life experiences, the people you wish to experience them with, and to utilise your gifts and abilities to experience the highest possible levels of joy. And you can also choose to give away this freedom of choice and free will by allowing others to dominate and dictate your life. By allowing yourself to be controlled, and by seeking permission and validation.

You may become anxious and confused when you allow others to control your choices and behaviour. You lose your sense of identity when you try to please others; afraid to be truly seen and heard, afraid to ask for what you want, just so that others don't feel threatened – and don't reject you.

It is imperative that you become assertive. This is not being dominant or pushy, or forcing your will onto others. Being assertive is coming from a place of quiet strength and dignity, standing firm in your decisions and choices of what is good for *you* – and not allowing the fears of others to direct the course of your life.

It can be painful to move on from people in your life, particularly if you cared deeply for them, or they hurt you in some way. If the connection was strong, it may be all the harder to cope with letting them go. Sometimes, even if there is anger and deep hurt, it's the *familiarity* of the person or their behaviour that is hard to let go of.

The truth is that not everyone who enters your life was ever meant to stay. Some people will enter your life to challenge you to heal your past. They will help you to recognise and release unhealthy behaviour, so that you stop repeating them once and for all. Perhaps you notice recurring patterns in your relationships? Perhaps they may even remind you of particular relationships; ones which had a profound impact on your life?

People will come in to help you to heal and move on from this. In a way, you hire each other to come together at the right time, under the right circumstances, to trigger something deep within you. This trigger is what comes up for examination and healing. And when the work is complete, some of these people will stay (perhaps as partners or friends) and you will continue this growth and life journey together. Others will leave your life altogether. This is not a reflection of your worth. It is simply as it was always meant to be. Accept the lesson. Bless what was, and let them go.

Notice where in your life you've become too safe, too secure. Where have things become routine, dull, even boring? In what way has your comfort zone become a trap? It's time to try new things, to achieve some new goals. Expand your territory. *Challenge yourself.* What would give you a massive sense of satisfaction and achievement?

When life becomes dull and routine, with nothing to stretch you, you get bored. Not much excites you, and this is where you begin to feel a lack of satisfaction and fulfillment, because all you are doing is what you already know. You begin to turn to others to supply you with the excitement you crave. And when they don't, you feel disappointed, let down and unloved. Or, you become tired and lose your sparkle. You wonder what happened to the person you used to be.

Notice the person you 'used' to be was likely often fearless. Notice you were the initiator. You were very tuned in with your flow and with your nature, and when you wanted to add something to your experience, you did. It was that simple.

Allow yourself to *not know*. Be okay with not knowing how things will work out. Allow yourself to relax into trusting that everything is unfolding exactly as it should. You are not always required to be an active participant. You may think that you know how things 'should' turn out, but this is only from your need for things to be easy and comfortable. Rarely will life unfold according to a specific plan.

Clinging to certainty only creates anxiety due to a need for control. It creates stress. And how can you control an outcome anyway? You have no control over other people; what they think, do and say. You have no idea what life has planned for you. The only thing within your control is you.

This is not to say you should sit back and do nothing. You *are* the creator of your life. Choose your target and aim to strike, but be flexible, be prepared to alter your trajectory if need be. Life is *supposed* to be filled with surprises and delights, so let go and allow the chips to fall where they may. They are going to anyway. You are well equipped to deal with whatever shows up. Release the need for control; for in truth, you are in control of very little. Practise spontaneity. Learn to enjoy life's surprises.

Focus on what will make your life even better. Stop living in the past, suspended in time. Turn and face forwards, for this is where you are heading. In what ways can you improve the quality of your life? What new beginnings might alter the fabric of your life?

You are a powerful creator, and you know this, so what are you creating? Is it a life of perpetuating heartache, confusion and regret, or is it powerful, inspiring and exciting? Are you able to step away from things and people who have long left your side, to focus on the business of being YOU? Are you able to open up to new opportunities for joy, abundance and love?

Do you have the courage to step into what fills you with the greatest purpose and fulfillment, and continue walking this path, *knowing that in doing so you are leaving your past behind?*

Value yourself, and your time on this planet, above all others. Don't treat it like a movie reel, as though you get a replay. Fill up your life so it is overflowing with joy. Extend your network of friends. Take up a completely new interest. Pick a topic and master it. Create a bucket list. Find a way to truly feel excited and inspired every day. This is it. This is your life, and life isn't happening 'some day', it's happening *now.*

Remind yourself that happiness is an inside job. It's not someone else's responsibility. Others will bring you joy, they will add to the richness of your life, but they are not responsible for your feelings. These belong to you. Happiness is created by you, for you. Of course there are elements that contribute to happiness, such as love, money, power, possessions, but are these true representations of happiness? Or are you really searching for safety and security? What is happiness?

Could it be feelings of joy spreading like warm silk throughout your body? Could it be laughter bubbling up from deep within? Is it knowing that you are perfectly capable of dealing with whatever life brings your way? Or that you have complete freedom to create your world any way you want it to be? Is happiness the power to govern yourself, and your life, any way you choose? If so, how is any of this dependant on an outside source?

Perhaps you might now stop giving others so much power over your life. Perhaps it is time for you to stop focusing on what others have not done for you. Ask yourself how you want to feel, and go about creating events and circumstances to allow them to show up in your life.

Search for evidence that abundance flows into your life, easily and effortlessly. Notice every single sign that shows you that you are on the right path. Shut down your default programming that has you silently expecting the worst, or thinking that nothing good could ever happen for you, or even searching for everything that could be wrong with a perfectly joyous and exciting event. What you go searching for is exactly what you will find.

Stop searching for all the 'wrong' in your life and begin to expect everything to work out well, because why would it not? Why should life not give you wonderful outcomes? Why would you not receive love, gifts, support, money, compliments, friendships, opportunities and joy? Why not you?

And in the face of all this abundance, why would you not accept and receive it all wholeheartedly? Expect things to work out well. Expect to receive blessings. Even despite outward appearances, expect that solutions will work in your favour. Just for fun, expect abundance to flow into your life, and it will indeed start showing up.

Notice any recurring patterns or themes in your life. Do you seem to attract the same sort of people, relationships, events and circumstances? If you are struggling with the same types of challenges and it seems the same scenarios are re-creating themselves over and over, it may be that you are missing the common denominator. You.

This is not to say you are to 'blame' in any way, there's no blame in the game of life, there are only the choices you make. But rather, something inside of you - perhaps subsonsciously, perhaps not - is needing the experience. And so you continue the pattern of thinking and behaviour that will ensure the experience arrives. Whether this experience is healthy for you or not is for you to decide. Is it time you learned this lesson and released it? Most likely.

The past is generally a pretty good predictor of the future, and life always leaves clues. It shouldn't be difficult for anyone to recognise what's looping in their life. We're all pretty good at discerning what is productive and what is destructive.

What is this experience giving you? Is it a sense of security, comfort, or even love? Can you not give yourself these things in other ways? A little courage and self-belief goes a long way. Try creating new patterns for yourself; patterns that give you feelings of power, strength and independence.

All it takes is one decision to change the entire course of your life. What's the one decision you've been putting off, knowing that this is true? What is the one decision, that if you made it, would change the direction of your life? And if you really want this change, and you know it's within reach, what have you been waiting for? Are you so comfortable in your current discomfort and pain?

Are you afraid of *how* it will change your life? Are you afraid of losing people? Of being in charge? Of making your own decisions? Of being on your own? Loss is always necessary when making room for change. There is always something – a person, job, residence, finances, *who you have been up to this point* – that must be released in order for things to be *different.* You don't get to change your life and yet retain everything in it and still be the same person, because then nothing has changed. It just doesn't work that way.

Of course big changes are frightening and should never be taken lightly. But if you have been feeling its pull, an inner knowing that this is what you must do, but you've been holding back out of fear, then you are in a fair bit of 'soul pain'. You're feeling torn. The only question is, is the pain of daring to change your life, to make it better, any worse than the pain of staying right where you are?

Notice the thoughts that pass through your mind. Notice whether they are kind thoughts, angry thoughts, worrying thoughts, or fearful thoughts. Notice how they make you feel. Notice how you respond to these thoughts. Notice how many thoughts you have. And then ask yourself: "Who is noticing all these thoughts?"

With practice, you will begin to understand that you are also the 'observer'. You will notice that the observer sits quietly, neutrally, without judgement or condemnation. While observing your thoughts, you will come to see that they are simply clouds passing across the windscreen of your mind.

You are not your thoughts. You are a person *having* a thought. You are not bad for having a bad thought. You are not weak for having a helpless thought. You are entertaining yourself with musings of the mind and made up stories. You will understand that you have the power to diffuse any emotionally painful thoughts; thoughts that trigger unpleasant emotional responses, simply by noticing that you are observing them. You are the observer, noticing the thoughts.

By now you've noticed that people will help you with your spiritual growth: they enter your life to hold up the mirror of your own patterns and behaviours so that you may heal and change them. But it is also true that many opportunities for growth simply cannot occur in the presence of others. We often reach a limit of growth surrounded by the same people.

These are the times when you may notice your friends have drifted away, or that you have completely new ones. Or that you are simply no longer compatible with people closest to you. *Nothing is challenging you to step up. Nothing is pushing you to grow. This requires a new level of experience.*

Sometimes this also requires periods of solitude. Time on your own. Some of your greatest insights and breakthroughs will occur when your space and energy isn't clouded by others.

This is your growth, right here. It is not a time to be fearful, but a time to get really, really excited. Your life is upgrading.

Only in solitude do you witness your true self. Only in solitude will you bump up against your greatest fears – and heal them. Only on your own will you discover your strengths and vulnerabilities. And through this self-discovery, a deep and profound sense of love and self-respect will emerge. *You know.* You know that whatever unfolds, whatever life has planned, you will be just fine.

Be the person who is a great example of integrity, self-trust and discipline. Keep your promises to yourself and to others. Build up your self-esteem by living in integrity. More than an exercise in honouring commitments, it's about earning respect – the respect of your spirit. It's trusting yourself to follow through. Being honest, truthful, reliable and dependable, so that others trust you as well.

Keeping your word is also even more than integrity. It's about who you become as a person - a clear thinker, great decision maker and confident in your own abilities.

Every time you break your word, a little piece of your soul gets chipped away. You let yourself down. After a while, you begin to doubt even yourself and it has a flow on effect. You may be slower to make decisions or to make any at all. You may find yourself going back and forth in indecision and confusion. Dig your heels in, make a commitment and stick with it. And then do it consistently until it becomes who you are. You might make some mistakes. Good! Mistakes are valuable; make them and make them fast. You're not doing it for the result itself, you're doing it for the promise to yourself.

Your word is powerful and says a lot about your character. This will influence the quality of people, and the quality of experiences, you will attract into your life.

How you define 'worthiness'? Is it being in some way deserving? Is it a measure of a hard earned prize? Is it defined by your appearance? Is it being good enough or loved and wanted? You are more than your human body, you are Divine Spirit in human form. You are worthy and deserving exactly as you are. Spirit is already good enough. There is nothing you need to do, no one else you need to be.

You compare yourself to others in the mistaken belief that if only you were as attractive, as rich, as talented, as 'lucky', you would have all you desire and be happy. There are many rich and attractive people in the world who are miserable. You limit yourself in the illusion that you are not lovable, that good things can't happen to you, that you're not free to express who you truly are and go after your wildest dreams, because, who would care? You feel insignificant; not worth anyone's time and attention.

There is no room for comparison. What if we all looked the same? What if we all had the same talents and abilities? It would be a world full of clones and how would we advance? How would there be innovation? How would we be different, contributing to the world in our many different ways?

You are YOU. Interesting, different, quirky, talented, beautiful, caring, loving, supportive, generous. You are more than worthy. You are utterly priceless.

Put aside your fears for the state of the world. Put aside wishing things were different, or better. For this is the world you came here to serve.

Life is not random. Your race, colour, and unique life circumstances are no accident. Nor is it an accident that you are alive *now*. You are an important part of the healing and transformation of the world and its people. You are alive because you are key to the changes and shifts that future generations will experience.

You are here to serve; helping people through healing, or through challenge. Put another way, you will assist others through inspiration, encouragement and reflection, or, you will assist them through pain and harm. One is desirable and the other is not, but both will push the soul to grow.

You may not know what your role is. You may not be aware of what talents and abilities you have to help facilitate these changes. You may feel it as a deep knowing that you are here for a reason; for greatness, for *more*, but you can't quite place your finger on what that is. It can be limiting and frustrating, but the nature of your service to the world will become clear to you once you are ready to acknowledge your gifts and begin to use them.

At any time, you have the solution. You always know what you need to do. It is fear that gives you the illusion of confusion, of 'not knowing', because that's a very convenient way to avoid doing something. Whether you need to end the relationship, quit the job, say no, or move cities, you always know exactly what needs to be done. And this can be a huge decision. It can be literally life changing, throwing everything into upheaval and turmoil.

You will search for answers outside of yourself. You will seek advice. You will prolong unhealthy situations, or wait for someone else to make the first move, or even force your hand. But, the dust will always settle. The time will come when the discomfort ends, and you will relax into the changes; safe, content and secure. Every storm passes, and so too will this.

Are you afraid of bearing the full weight of responsibility for the decision you make? Are you afraid of making the wrong decision? Can it take you on a different path? Can it remove you from a situation of pain and suffering? Can it give you more opportunity to improve your life? The thing about making wrong decisions, is that you don't know they're wrong until you make them. Up until then you're just anticipating an outcome and making assumptions, which may or may not be correct.

It will be most helpful for you to focus more on what you have to *gain*, and less on what you have to lose.

The truth is that you will never experience the world as it truly is; you can only ever experience it from your own perspective.

You will only see the world through the lens of your personal beliefs, experience, thoughts and opinions. If you are a generally fearful and pessimistic person, then you will perceive the world as a fearful place, with much to distrust. If on the other hand, you are of a positive, open and adventurous nature, you will find the world to be full of beauty, joy and pleasurable experiences. Same world, different perspectives. Which one is true?

In the same way, the events in your life are deeply personal. What you believe to be a hurtful rejection may, for others, mean the redirection to something better, and therefore, a blessing. When people have different interpretations, they will arrive at differing conclusions. Who is right and who is wrong?

Can you co-exist in harmony with contrasting points of view? Can you drop your need to be right, and become open to learning? Can you simply be okay that not everyone agrees with you? After all, it's these very differences that make conversations so stimulating and enjoyable. The alternate points of view. The discovery of something new. The dawning of understanding.

It was the Dalai Lama who once said, "Sometimes, not getting what you want is a marvellous stroke of luck".

Have you ever really wanted something, but were redirected to something even better? Have you repeatedly knocked on the same door and it refused to open? Have you mourned the loss of a relationship, only to find out later it was the best thing that could have happened? Life always knows what needs to happen. It always has a better plan. And only in retrospect can you see that this is true.

It's important to have goals and dreams, things that inspire you and get you excited about life. It's great to have plans. But there are times when the thing you want is very likely to take you right off path. Or, it may even have the potential to do you harm.

It could be a relationship you really want, a promotion, or to travel the world. It seems easy enough, but you come up against roadblock after roadblock. It begins to seem impossible to achieve, expecially when nothing is lining up in your favour. And this is your clue. What is 'right' for you may take some effort, but it shouldn't be too hard. Unless it's not right for you. In which case, you may have just dodged a bullet.

Know that once you have firmly set an intention or a desire, it is done. Such is your power. It is already waiting to manifest for you as your physical reality. There is no need to repeatedly ask for it, pray for it or beg for it. You were heard the first time. Your job now is to expect it. Receive it. Allow it into your life. Start looking for evidence of its manifestation, no matter how big or small. No matter the form it takes.

You *do not* receive anything with an ungrateful thought or response. You *do not* brush off anything as being a coincidence or random occurrence. Start paying attention to clues. Manifestation begins immediately; usually with little signs, to test your willingness to receive what you claim you want.

Have full expectation of its presence in your life. Do not concern yourself with how or when. Know that you will be guided and inspired to make decisions and choices which will pave the way for your desire to fully show up at the right time, in the most perfect way for you.

You can also stop second guessing yourself, whether you are worthy of it, whether your request is too big, too greedy, too much… this kind of thinking will stop it dead in its tracks. Be honest with what you want. And have absolute faith and belief that it will show up.

When it seems as though your every effort is consistently blocked - as though everything is a struggle, as though all you are doing is just pushing - it can feel like you're spinning your wheels. It's utterly exhausting. Life will test you, most definitely. It will test your endurance: are you willing to do what must be done, as long as it takes? It will test your patience: are you willing to release control? It will test your authenticity: is this really what you want?

Above all, life will test you to trust that everything is unfolding exactly as it should. It's asking you to just step back; you've got to allow your manifestation to take place. It's telling you that you can only start things moving along; you cannot force them into being. Perhaps life is reminding you to remain humble. Perhaps you are being reminded to be wary of your own arrogance. Life will test you when you think you can do it all alone. You cannot. It will test you when you think you can bend the laws of the Universe to suit you. You will not. It will test you when you are headed in the wrong direction, with gentle prompting and subtle signs.

Perhaps life is really not testing you at all. Perhaps in keeping you away from potentially unhealthy relationships and potentially damaging outcomes, it is protecting you. Perhaps life really deserves your gratitude for sparing you.

The only thing that will ever come between you and your goals is your lack of clarity. That's it. It's not time or money or talent. You are simply not seeing the end result you are after. With clarity, your pathway is a clear one. Not always easy, but clear. You understand what you need to do and you do it. You find out what you need to learn and you learn it. You recognise who can help you and you get help.

Sometimes you will find yourself wanting to do something and in the process you begin to find excuses, think it's too hard, or frequently get busy doing other, totally unimportant and insignificant things. You do everything you can to avoid what you know you need to do. You do this for the simple reason that you are not clear on the outcome. You are not clear on what you are doing, or why you are doing it.

This procrastination strategy will fall away completely once you know exactly what your goal is. Be exceptionally clear on what you want and why you want it, and you will begin to see the next step and then the next. As if by magic, the veils will begin to part, and insights, ideas and inspiration will all come flooding in, as well as the desire and motivation you need to achieve it.

Most people will say that their goal is "Just to be happy". This isn't enough. Of course you want to be happy but happiness in itself cannot be a goal. Constant and never-ending happiness would very quickly become a boring and tiresome burden, for where is the contrast? Where is the challenge? What are you striving towards? Life comes in many different shades and does include anger, sadness, pain, failure, and disappointment, and it is these very shades that allow you to experience and appreciate their opposite - what you define as happiness.

It is your undesired feelings that give you the impetus and momentum to keep moving forward and striving for better. Painful feelings are what push you forward. They are your indicator that something is wrong and that you need to do something to make it right.

Is it not your feelings of sadness that move you towards a quality of living that brings you joy? Is it not loneliness that drives you out of your comfort zone, into the world, to connect with new people and make new friends? Is it not your anger that spurs you on to take charge of your life? Happiness is a result of inspired living, of growth, of adventure, of daring to take risks, of loving, completely and utterly. It's not enough to want happiness; you need to take the journey, fight your demons, gather some battle scars, and emerge triumphant, ecstatic and feeling fully alive.

How do you want your life to look? What do you want to be doing? Who do you want to be doing it with? What are your plans for the next five years? The next decade? What legacy will you leave behind? How will you be remembered? It's a lot to think about (and most people spend more time planning their holiday), but have you ever asked yourself these questions?

The fact is, these things are going to happen whether you are consciously driving them or not. You will be doing something with your life (whether you love it or not), you will be doing it with someone (whether you choose the right person or settle for who you get), you will be getting up for something every day (whether it's a fulfilling and stimulating career or you drift from one job to another), you will have plans for the next ten years (plans for achievement or no plans at all), and you will leave a legacy and be remembered (for whatever you chose to do and whoever you chose to be).

The difference is that either life just 'happens' to you – or - you can decide how you are going to spend your limited time. You are a powerful creator and with focused intention there is almost nothing you cannot create. Simply think about the lifestyle you desire. What will support this? What type of person lives like this? What do they do? How can you create this for yourself?

You created your life, as it is, right now. And you did most of it without any conscious awareness. What do you think you can achieve with deliberate intention and focus?

You have knowledge and expertise. You have talents and skills that are uniquely your own. You have remarkable gifts that will help others. Do not second guess your value to the world. Who you are, and what you have, needs to be shared. You may at times feel the pull to explore these gifts or even reveal them to others, but you hold back, afraid of being judged. You question your own value, whether you can be any help at all. You may wonder what one person can do. Everything starts with one person.

What if you knew that you had the power to change just one person's life? What if you knew that you could change a person's day, just by helping to lift their mood? Or that maybe, someone held onto life a little longer because you gave them hope? Isn't it selfish to keep these gifts to yourself? If you could help others, why would you not?

It is all too easy to become a wallflower; keeping yourself small, unnoticed and insignificant. It's like flying under the radar. Only you have a duty – all of us do – to take responsibility for helping to shape the world. To help your fellow humans, if you can. Those who reject their gifts only fear what they do not understand. They only reject what is in themselves. So, help them understand. Help them to accept themselves. And in helping them, you will begin to help yourself.

Not much in life is worthwhile without appreciation. Be grateful for everything that shows up in your life. The joys, the hardships, and everything in between. For they have all contributed and combined to bring you to this very moment in time. Be grateful for what you already have, and it will very quickly multiply.

Even though at times things may seem difficult, take a moment to also look around you and give thanks; someone else in the world is facing trials and hardships of the likes you've never seen. Always show gratitude to others, for what they have done for you, and for what they have brought into your life.

Tell someone you love them

Send them a handwritten card

Acknowledge their efforts

Thank them for all they've done

Encourage them in their own pursuits

Help them achieve their goals

Perform a spontaneous service

Let them know they matter

It's not enough to live with hope and good intentions. You have to act. The only way to see change is to do things repeatedly and consistently. Trust yourself enough to make the right decisions for you and then have the confidence to follow through. Life is a fine dance between taking action on your dreams and desires, and knowing when to pull back to allow what needs to unfold. Amidst all of this, you are constantly thinking. Thinking about what you want, what you don't have, your fears, duties and obligations. You are thinking your life into reality.

What you do as a result of your thoughts creates your reality. What you do not do creates your reality. Do you realise that either way, you are creating your reality?

Life doesn't change because you sat in fifteen minutes of focused intention, chanting or affirmations. Or because you glued some pictures onto a vision board. It won't change simply because you told yourself that it must. It changes because you did something to change your outcomes. You did something different. And you did things habitually and consistently, every single day.

It is important to make the distinction between your life and your life's circumstances. It can be easy to become disenchanted and anxious when you look around and find things are less than ideal. It is easy to think that 'this' is all that you amount to.

Whether these are poor quality relationships, debt, a job you hate, or even if you simply don't like your life, know that these are only situations. These are events that are going on in your current reality. And these can change.

However, they do not define who you are. You are not the house mortgage, the divorce or the illness. For that matter, you are not your huge salary, your promotion, or your happy home. Nothing outside of you has any bearing on who you are. You are the size of your heart. You are the kindness in your soul. You are the smile that lights up the world. You are your intentions, your generosity, your compassion. You are powerful and joyous and courageous, and you can change your external world to reflect your internal one anytime you wish.

Don't confuse the two. Your circumstances are where you find yourself at the moment, and they can and are prone to change. Who you are is your soul – eternal, and always wonderful.

Once upon a time, you thought that the older you got, the wiser you became. That at some point you would become clearer on who you were and where you were going. That you would become stronger, more confident and self-assured. That you would develop a clear direction, mission and set of goals, all of which would usually revolve around a solid career, spouse, children and a regular holiday destination.

You never imagined there would be doubt. You never imagined there would be questions, insecurity, and uncertainty. That there would be fear, stress and worry. That you would often wonder who you are, and how you got to this point.

Because, aren't you supposed to have all your ducks lined up by now? Isn't that what everyone does? There is good news, and good news. The good news is that no one has it all worked out; we're all grappling along in the dark, making it up as we go. The other good news is that life is a moving target; always fluid, never static. Which means we're all constantly changing, learning and adapting. We're making great choices and bad choices, and none of them are really wrong choices.

Some people nail their careers straight off, but don't do so well in relationships. Others avoid commitment of any kind and choose to roam the world, learning and exploring. Life is not a fixed plan; it is what you choose for yourself and how you choose to live it. There is no yardstick by which you should be measured. Arrive where you need to be, whenever you need, to be there.

Be uplifting and inspiring. Be outspoken. Be outrageous. Smile often and engage in conversation. Help others. Show kindness, care and love. Right now, the world needs more fabulous, the world needs more captivating, the world needs more inspiring and interesting, the world needs more laughter and love – this is your gift; do not hide it away or modify it. Please do not settle for less than you are. You have the power to create ripples in the world around you.

There is no such thing as an ordinary day or an ordinary moment. Start treating every single minute as miraculous – it is! Anything and everything can happen in the blink of an eye. Your entire life circumstances can completely change. Every single moment of your life should be treated with respect.

Live as though you mean it. Give the benefit of your experience and wisdom. Be a guide, an advisor, a mentor. Be a catalyst. Have an opinion. Stand for something. Be the person everyone wants to be around because of how you make them feel. Be open to learning and be happy to be wrong. Take a chance on a new venture, on being rejected, on living a dream. Get out of your home, your environment, your circle of friends, and do something different. Scatter good will everywhere and leave your fabulous footprint on the planet.

Never allow yourself to fall into the 'as good as it gets' mind trap. There is always a higher quality version of everything in life and you are worthy of this. You may at times feel low self-esteem, low self-worth, or conscious of age and the passing of time, so you take whatever comes your way, just in case it's your 'last chance'. You may be in the midst of a situation that seemed wonderful to begin with and now the cracks are starting to appear… it's not as nice or as healthy as you first thought. And yet, you choose to stay, because it's there. Or you simply can't be bothered starting all over again.

Do not allow temporary feelings of disillusionment to lock you into a false sense of entrapment. 'Settling' is comfortable and doesn't ask much of you. It doesn't hold you to any particular standards, and never asks you to step up in your life. For a while it may seem fine to cruise along at this altitude, but one day, you feel the pain, the deep yearning, the knowing that things could have been different. This is the pain of years with someone you never really loved (or even liked). Or years in a job you loathed. Even worse, it shows up as massive pain for a life full of potential, but never realised.

Expect more of yourself, and of life. Show the same level of respect and thought to the choices that will influence the course of your life, as you do when shopping for clothes. Get a feel for it. Try it on. If you don't like it, put it back and find something more suitable.

It's a curious thing, isn't it? You search your memories from events long passed; willingly reliving them, willingly causing yourself pain. It's as though you think that by going back, something will be different. Or that you will find something you had previously overlooked that will make you feel better. But nothing is different. The event is the same. It's always the same pain. The same regret. The same anger. Only because you keep going there, the attachment becomes stronger; the event hasn't changed but your feelings towards it become more and more painful.

You allow this memory to become a strong reference point which affects your future. Every new opportunity gets compared against what happened 'last time' and so without realising it, you have already judged and dismissed a potentially stunning new chapter in your life. Or at the very least, your feelings of pain are trapped inside your body, unresolved, with nowhere to go, and you wonder why you feel unwell. It's time for peace. Do not drag your past into your present.

You have every opportunity right now to create a different future, but you have got to stop looking behind you, accept what occurred (what choice do you really have?) and focus on yourself. Build yourself UP. Create a life to look forward to; you can do this, everyone can, but some people just can't be bothered. Be bothered.

It takes focus and discipline, and re-training your thinking, but if you can create in your mind a compelling vision of your future, and a genuine desire to succeed, before you know it, there will be so much change you will not recognise your life.

Look ahead. Make some plans. Set new goals. Go the distance. Don't ever become too comfortable once you've reached a certain age or have acquired everything you think you want from life. There is no finish line. Keep moving, growing, stretching and learning. Continue to challenge yourself, your beliefs, abilities and potential achievements. Learn about the world around you. Move away from your interests and what you already know; there's no challenge for growth there. Read up on topics you normally have no interest in, for a different perspective. Read autobiographies of random people and learn through the experiences of others.

Do things that are uncomfortable and even scary. Create fresh new experiences. Find out what thrills you, and connect with new people along the way. Stop focusing so much on self-improvement; get out of your head, out of your worries and dramas, and focus outwards. What more can you learn? What more can you do? How can you get out into the world and feel alive?

Change your routine. Greet the sun. Feel the pain. Laugh at bad jokes. Say 'yes' to desires of your time and 'no' to demands. Be bold. Speak with those people who are living your dream. Ask them to help you get there. Life rewards those who help themselves. Who ask for what they want and are willing to reach out; unapologetic about their dreams.

Do you remember what you received for your birthday two years ago? You probably don't and not many people do. How about your holiday from ten years ago? Quite likely you remember most of it in vivid detail. Focus your intentions towards collecting memories, not things. Of course you have basic physical needs for everyday living, and it's good to strive for nice things. There is nothing at all wrong with that. But it's your memories that give you the greatest joys in life. This is a treasured gift that lives on forever.

You won't cuddle your brand new car when you feel sad, but you will curl up and think of happier times. You will remember people fondly by getting lost in days of fun and adventure. And they will help you to push forward when times are tough. What else does creating memories mean? It means you've done some pretty amazing things! You dared to live!

It's fun times with friends and family, playing with your children, connecting with those around you. It's doing risky things, crazy things, conquering your fears. It's feeling the broad spectrum of everything – happiness, sadness, love, fear, excitement, and pain. It's living life ALL IN, and having stories to share for years to come.

Your life is a mystery, as indeed so are you. Notice that although you surround yourself with things, with people, although you have spent a lifetime acquiring knowledge, there is still an unsatisfied hunger within you. Perhaps you do not know what it is you search for. Perhaps your deep yearning is a clue.

You seek deeper meaning and fulfillment. You seek your role, your place. You seek to understand yourself beyond your surface level, and going deep within this level is the only place you will begin to find answers. It is not to be found in the thoughts and opinions of others. It is not even found in the teachings of others, for, consider this: What are your teachers really teaching you other than truth from their own perspective? What are they teaching you but lessons handed down from teacher to student over many generations? All valuable information, to be sure, but you may call it recycled information. The same knowledge repeated over and over in the name of truth; but whose truth?

The answers you seek - your own truth - are only found within you. It is the only place for you to go. You are the only mystery you need to solve.

At times you will feel so alone; alone with your sadness. Alone with your fears. You will feel so sensitive, so fragile. And you will notice that throughout these moments, all you seek is yourself. You don't want anyone around you. You don't want the intrusion on your energy. You simply need you. You may feel abandoned. You may feel as though you've prayed, you've asked, you've begged, over and over, for things to improve, for better than this. And yet, things still remain the same. You lose faith, you lose all belief in being loved and cared for by a benevolent universe.

Can you allow yourself to trust that you have been heard, and that change is already in motion? Can you hold on a little longer? Here's why: change doesn't happen with the sweep of one big cataclysmic event. And this is how you believe your prayers will be answered; this is what you are waiting for. But things rarely ever change this way, because the force of such a massive change would be too unsettling and ungrounding. Although it does happen. And people rarely have a great time with it.

Look around you for small incremental changes, for this is where things begin their shift. Notice the little things; the evidence that crops up all around you. They will be synchronicities, random words or opportunities, a person who suddenly appears, an offer out of the blue. It could also be sudden guidance or inspired action. Every prayer is answered, but too often we are busy ignoring the signs to notice.

You exert so much energy trying to not be you. You spend lifetimes trying to ignore and suppress your darker aspects, those parts that make up your whole. You speak ill of yourself, treat yourself terribly, despising those parts you perceive to be 'lacking'. You even treat some aspects of yourself as a 'dirty little secret' or something to be deeply ashamed of. You abuse yourself, ignore yourself, are cruel to yourself…and yet it is you. You do all of this to yourself.

These aspects could be an addiction, an over-eater, a procrastinator. They may have stolen, lied or broken someone's heart. They are a part of you that is ever in the background, crying out for love. Notice how you try to keep them suppressed and controlled? How you pretend they don't exist? They are the child that stomps its feet in a tantrum when ignored. That appears, right on time, to sabotage a good thing.

They are the boiling pot about to blow its lid. You move cities, even countries to escape them, yet wherever you go… there they are.

You are taught that you are broken and need fixing. You are never broken. There is nothing to fix. You need your own love and acceptance. You need to accept that you have a dark side, because everybody does. Acknowledge how often it helps you by giving you a balanced perspective of your life. It only surfaces when it's in pain, wanting your attention. So don't ignore it. Ask it what it needs. And then give it that.

Observe carefully those around you, for they are your teacher. Some are already walking the path which you are, right now, considering for yourself; observe their results, for they have saved you time. Some have taught you the cost of indulging in addictions and foolish behaviour; they have lost everything. Observe their results, for they have saved you heartache. Some have pushed you and tricked you and lied to you, and forced you to face what is necessary in your life; be grateful for their cruelty. They have improved you.

The soul craves knowledge, and knowledge is gained from experience. When your soul desires knowledge, it will create the experience required. You will literally manifest the lesson. But you don't always need to go through painful lessons; you can acquire knowledge simply by observing others, and learning from their outcomes, for they are your teachers.

And thank them, even when they do you wrong. Even when they hurt you, they are supporting your growth. Look back upon your life and see that this is true. Notice how you emerged from all of your experiences. Notice that every one of them shone a light on what was previously hidden. Every experience exposed that of which you were unaware.

Consider the Universe for a moment. By virtue of it's own creation - gravity - it keeps the planets hanging at a safe distance, up in space. It turns tiny acorns into massive oak trees. It dictates changing seasons and the wonders of nature. It is a force of stunning magnitude, so why do you show it such a lack of trust, impatience and fear? You do this when you refuse to allow what is. When you fear that what you want won't arrive the way you want it. When you try to force your desired outcomes and bend life to your will. All you get from this is anxiety and dead ends. You exert so much energy and mental stamina trying to force things into being that it's exhausting.

The Universe delivers in its own time. It knows the entire blueprint of your life and it knows better than you what you must experience. Do you think that you have a better plan than the Universe? Life is about co-creation. That's the two of you working together. Your job is to uncover your gifts and talents and use them. To bring them out into the world in a way that is useful and beneficial. And along the way, you will be guided to stay on course.

Resisting the Universe is like trying to control the uncontrollable. Work with what is presented to you, trusting that something greater is unfolding. If you don't like it, change it, and then work with that. Like a flowing river, always be moving along with the current.

Would you rather kid yourself and feel joyous, vibrant and alive, or kid yourself and feel hopeless, bitter and depressed? Positivity. Optimism. Affirmations. Sometimes you may think that this is all a load of fluff. That you're kidding yourself. After all, where is the evidence that any of this works? Well, there's no evidence at all. It may all be made up nonsense. But, if holding a positive mindset, expecting good out of every outcome, repeating affirmations and staying generally optimistic makes you feel good, feel better about your life and your circumstances, then why would you not? Where's the harm?

You may say it's not being 'realistic', but how is constant complaining and a negative attitude any more realistic? If anything, these attitudes will create even more challenges for you. Why?

Because complaining is saying that nothing is ever good enough. That it should be different, that there is a lack – it's opposite. So you're focused on lack. And you get more lack. Complaining puts you in a negative state, it makes you angry, as though everything is conspiring against you. How do you enjoy life with this attitude? How do you see the beauty in the world around you, in the eyes of your loved ones, in the faces of your friends? And speaking of friends. Who will find you a pleasure to be around?

When you start losing motivation and the desire is fading away, all it takes is a small shift in perception to refocus your energy. Keep up your momentum by focusing on commitment, rather than motivation. Motivation is more or less a feeling, and your feelings change every day. When you're feeling super charged and good about yourself, it's easy to keep going; anyone can do this. But the true test is when your mood is low, when you struggle to see the good in anything. Here is where the motivation dips, when you can't be bothered. Staying motivated anyway is hard, and not everyone can do this. In fact, this is where most people give up.

So, instead of making your life's decisions based on how you feel at the time, (which is pretty much how motivation works) focus instead on your commitment. Don't ask yourself how to keep going, ask yourself why you must. When you rely on motivation alone to see you through, there will be long periods of not much happening. Even though you can go through the motions mechanically, once your mind begins to check out, you are pretty much about to give up.

The trick to keeping your mind in the game is to constantly remind yourself of why you want 'it' in the first place. The issue is then no longer about remaining motivated, because not doing what you need to do is not even an option. Your comittment to your 'why' is what will get you over the line.

Like a revolving door, life will always follow a cycle, bringing you the good and the not-so-good. It's the natural order of things, just like the sun and the moon, day and night. It spins between joyful highs and painful lows, with plateaus in between. You might say that when you are experiencing a low phase in your life and nothing seems to go your way, your 'high' point is already in the making. Likewise, when you are experiencing great times and everything is going well, your 'low' point is also already in the making.

This is not a depressing thought, it is a comforting one. Nothing is eternal. Joy doesn't last forever and neither does pain. Life just cycles and balances out. It is what it is. Your attitude will have a lot to do with it. How you choose to accept the events may tip the scales in your favour; in which case, you will experience more joy. Due to your positive and accepting nature, you can choose to view anything as a good thing, or at the very least, you can choose to see that the outcome somehow worked in your favour.

This is not to say that just as you are enjoying a 'win' you can expect a sudden downturn in fortune. Not at all. But it is fairly realistic to say that there will at times, be disappointments. Expect this. And accept them just as equally as you would the joys.

Be mindful of making false assumptions, as they will lead you to take false actions. Misunderstandings will occur when you get lost in what you think the other person is trying to say. Assuming what they are thinking and feeling will create a whole new storyline in your head – an entirely one sided perception.

Do not pre-judge the situation; instead, listen with an open heart. Allow yourself to gently move from a place of needing to be 'right', to loving empathy where you are not thinking about what words you need to say next, because you are immersed in listening. Let them open up and let them feel safe in speaking from a place of honesty and vulnerability.

You will not hear their perspective, their truth, if you are primed for attack. Or, if your mind is clouded with prejudgements, for your focus is only on yourself. Your focus is only on how you feel you have been wronged.

Be honest in your communication with others too, for they may also take 'false action' based upon their false assumptions. Don't just say what you think they want to hear; you need to speak your truth and they need to hear this truth. It all seems like an awful lot of trouble that could be easily avoided by simply being a grown up about life. Tell the truth. Don't play games. Assume nothing. Listen carefully.

A seed buried deep in the ground has no concept of itself. It has no idea how big it can become. No idea in which direction it will grow. Until it has begun its ascent, breaking through the surface of the soil, it can never know its potential. Until then, it is nestled in darkness, all alone.

You are this seed. You have greatness inside of you; brilliance of which you are unaware, nestled alone in your darkness. Right now, you may have no idea of what or who you will become. You have no idea how large you can grow. You think you have but one clear and straight path, but the truth is, you have the potential to go in any direction.

Once you begin to grow, to ascend, you will be influenced. As the plant will always begin to face the direction of the sun, you will also begin to gravitate towards that which feeds your soul and makes you feel alive. It may be people you are moving towards, or it may be the best possible circumstances for you. But it is always what fuels and nourishes your further growth.

How big can you become? That will be dependent on external factors as well, but it will come down to strength. How deep are your roots? How firm is your core? How thick is your skin? You are not unlike the humble seed. You will both grow. But where one will 'need to know', and will question everything, it will stunt and delay its own growth. The other will simply allow what is, and gracefully unfold.

When I bless others, I bless myself, and this is true. When you are sending goodwill to others - in thought or words - your subconscious thinks you are speaking of yourself. When you admire someone's work, or their appearance, or any positive characteristic, again, your subconscious thinks you are speaking of yourself. Why does it feel so good to compliment or lift others up? It feels good because the essence of your kind and beautiful thoughts have come straight back to you. When I bless others, I bless myself.

Pure and loving intention will raise your vibration. It will literally take you to a state of joy. Like attracts like. When you are feeling joy, you will attract more joy. You are telling the universe, "I want more of that!". When I bless others, I bless myself.

That place inside your heart, that expansiveness you feel when you pour your loving truth into another, will open you up. It will teach you to be receptive to receiving loving grace yourself. You begin to open to blessings in your life; noticing them, accepting them, thanking them. When I bless others, I bless myself. How can you not? You are blessing reflections of yourself, everywhere you turn.

You are manifesting your future, right now, whether you are aware of it or not. You are, right now, shifting, changing and re-arranging future events, although from your current vantage point you cannot see that this is the case. You may even be doubtful because you've asked for your desire and nothing has 'happened'. Well, here is the key to understanding the nature of manifestation: nothing happens without the participation of at least one other individual. You want a partner? You need a willing individual. You want a promotion? You need a boss to promote you.

So the events that will need to happen, and the people who will be called in to play their part for YOUR manifestations to occur, all need to be ordered and sequenced, while at the same time, they are also dealing with the arrangements for their own manifestations.

In other words, on an invisible and energetic level, a whole lot of lives need to collide, mesh and disperse again, at specific points in time. And this is happening continuously. It's a monumental web and we are closely tied in together. When you complain about 'nothing happening', just hold on; it is coming together, but take a step back and consider the task at hand.

We are all interconnected. And billions of people (energies, all over the world) are choosing and changing their realities every single day, and energies are constantly shifting and re-arranging. So, trust. It truly is not your job to worry about how things will unfold for you, for knowing this would blow your mind. Just trust that it will.

Find balance in moderation. You are equally a spiritual and a human being. You will discover your truth in the noise of life, nature, and other people, just as you will in hours of silence, solitude and meditation. The answers are within you, to be sure, however they are also found in life. The very things you perhaps try to avoid are the very things that will heighten your awareness, perception and recognition.

How else do you recognise that you are love, without the human experience which illuminates your acceptance and tolerance? How else do you recognise yourself as compassion until life gives you an experience in which there is no other way but to be compassionate?

It is life that shows you who you are. Quiet moments of introspection may clear your mental space and allow you glimpses of your soul, it may clear the way for peaceful contemplation and solutions, but it is life that provides the lessons. Spiritual practices are all powerfully valuable. Yet an overbalance becomes an excuse to hide.

You did not choose to return so that you could isolate yourself from the world, in separation from other human beings. Your purpose was to seek knowledge and understanding through your interaction with other souls. You had full awareness that you would experience life in all its flavours, and that you would learn of love and kindness, and hatred and pain. And you agreed to learn all of this while enjoying your human existence.

These experiences of the soul cannot occur when you are protecting yourself. They occur in total and complete vulnerability and innocence. In being willing to say, "This experience may bring me the greatest joy, or it may inflict the deepest pain, but either way, I need to know".

Only you can decide who you are, because you are who you say you are. Imagine for a moment you see yourself as fit, healthy and strong. Because this is how you see yourself, and therefore these beliefs are taking root, you will naturally gravitate towards doing the things that a fit person does – you will eat nourishing and nutritious foods, you will exercise, and enjoy an active lifestyle.

You don't wait until you actually are fit healthy and strong to do these things, because it's doing these things that will get you there. You step into the role, as you are now, and begin living your life as though you were already there, and soon enough you actually will be. If you see yourself as a powerful and successful individual, you will do what powerful and successful individuals do – become a clear thinker, make quick decisions, raise your standards for yourself, become a source of knowledge and help for others and always continue to learn and grow. If you wait until you become one, well, when do you become one? When do you start taking the steps required to get there? You see yourself that way first. It is not the other way around.

Don't complicate life. Everything begins with just one decision. Once your focus has shifted and is attuned to change, you step into the role of actively changing your life. You may begin looking for a new job, a new house, or you may undergo a radical change in your presentation and appearance which attracts an entirely new experience.

None of which could happen without first seeing yourself as the person you want to be. And after that decision, you step into the role and begin doing what 'that kind of person' would do.

When life isn't going so well, it's hard to be patient for better things to come along. You want things immediately, right now. The relationship, the money, the job, the one magical thing that will change your life forever. You don't want to hear that everything will come to you 'at the right time' or in 'perfect timing', because you need the change now, right? As far as you're concerned, now IS the perfect time.

Perfect timing is not when you happen to have made space in your life for something. It's when you've become the person you need to be to have it. It's when everything (and everyone) involved has aligned and caught up at the same intersection in time.

Let's say you want a relationship. You are so very ready to pour out your love and devotion, and to share your life with the right person. You're ready, perhaps also a little lonely.

You wonder what is wrong with you that you cannot attract a mate. Why is it taking so long? Perhaps, your intended partner is not yet ready for you. Perhaps they are still in the midst of separation from another. Or they may be still healing from their own hurt. Or alternatively, perhaps your current emotional state would attract someone very, very wrong for you.

What about the job you were hoping for? Your destiny was not in that role, otherwise it would be yours. And this is the truth. What IS right for you, and will set the foundation for your future success, is being orchestrated for you now, to arrive at the right time – when you are ready, and more importantly, when you are ready for the lessons it will bring.

What else is trust but strong belief and unwavering certainty? Trust sounds a lot like faith, but they are not the same. With faith you believe without evidence, and so it is 'supernatural' in nature. Your faith is that hope will be delivered through the intervention of a higher power. With trust on the other hand, you have a certain expectation, based on evidence (a person or an event), and you have full belief that your expectation will be met.

In difficult times, you will be called upon to show both. You will need to maintain your faith; your belief that life has a higher intention unfolding for you, and also your trust; most especially, trust in yourself and your ability to handle life.

Unfortunately, you cannot live on faith alone — even with the best of intentions. You must learn to trust yourself and your capabilities. You must learn to trust the decisions you make. You must seek outside of yourself less, and trust in your own instincts, more. How do you do this? You stand by your decisions. You don't go back and forth; you stand firm and back yourself. No second guessing. You trust your instincts and intuition. You act, or don't act, based upon what they are telling you. This is how you build up trust in yourself in the first place – by following your own instructions.

And when the storm rolls in (and it inevitably will), this is your test. Not to go scrambling; seeking external validation that you made the right choices, or that all will be well. Not to coerce, or beg and plead. Not to place yourself on the bargaining table. To simply trust.

Intuition is more than just a gut feeling. Yes it will give you a sense, an impression, of something or someone. But it is more than this. It is your absolute entire guidance system. Your intuition is telling you where you are off balance within your life and what needs your attention. It's not a particularly special gift; we are all born with it, but mostly we brush it off as a spiritually romantic gift. That the more spiritual our lives, the more intuitive we are. That it's like being psychic. No. Everyone is intuitive. And if used correctly it will allow you to successfully navigate your life.

Your intuition will show you how balanced your life is. How? Via your feelings, moods and physical symptoms. When you are feeling tense, anxious, sad or depressed, you are being shown that there is a part of your life you need to address. And although you pretend that you don't, you always know what that is. Likewise, when you're feeling fabulous and on top of the world, you are being shown what a balanced life looks like, and this is what you are striving to feel as much as possible.

Physical pains and symptoms will also provide you with answers. Is the pain in your power centre, your solar plexus? And are you feeling a loss of power in your life? Are you giving your power away? Is the pain around your back? Do you feel unsupported? Is it your throat area, and are you having trouble expressing yourself and speaking your truth? This is all coming through your intuition, specifically pointing you to the precise location of your imbalance.

And when you are living your life incongruently; perhaps doing something you really don't want to do, saying things that just aren't true, or ignoring a repetitive message coming through, it won't sit well. It's that uncomfortable feeling, when something is 'off'. This is also your intuition, reminding you that you have moved out of integrity.

Everybody wants to know their life purpose, as perhaps you may too. But understand what you are asking for. Your life's purpose is not a label. It's not to be found in a tidy job description that suddenly makes your existence worthwhile. If it's not a label then what is it? It is YOU. You are your life's purpose, your purpose is to be yourself. How can it not be? How can being the full embodied spirit that you are, with your own unique abilities and talents, passions, interests and influence on the planet NOT be your purpose for being here?

Think about what you are most passionate about. What do you think or do, at least once a day, every single day? How is doing or being this a natural extension of yourself? What gnaws away at you relentlessly? What won't go away? What did you think about and desire a year ago and still will, in another year? What is the one thing you just can't forget?

Your life's purpose is fulfilling that one thing you need to do, which is in full alignment with who you are. What is NOT your life's purpose? Anything that you begin to justify and explain away – not having the money or the time or 'it's just not possible for you'. This is where you've left your heart and gone into your head, and are most likely chasing something because you 'should'. What is true for you comes from your heart and you never stop to question it.

At some point in your life you may find yourself in a strange place. You're in a place of nothingness; a void. Possibly, you have just lost something very meaningful in your life. Or perhaps you have just lost everything. This void is the bridge between the past and your future. It's like having your arms outstretched in both directions with nothing to grasp onto. In panic you try to hold onto the past, but it has dissolved away. In fear you try to grab onto some kind of hope for the future but there is nothing there. The future has yet to come.

It feels like a suspension between two worlds and nothing is familiar. It's just you and surrender. And there is nothing for you to do but ride it out. Just let it all unfold. You can make it easier by being willing to stop fighting it, by keeping your mind strong with daily journaling and immersing yourself in more of what feels good for you. You can also feel more grounded and connected by daily practises such as exercise, yoga, meditation, gardening, or walking barefoot on the soil.

Right now, you are being called upon to open yourself in a way that you have never been called to before - to trust. Believe that things will be okay. They will be okay. Right now, you cannot possibly conceive of what is preparing itself for you, and you will rush towards it in joy when it becomes apparent.

Life changes can be very exciting, if you choose to see it that way. A new YOU, a new direction and a new way of being. Although they can seem large, looming and terrifying, it only appears this way because you feel you have no control. Remain curious. Remain the observer. Be ready to act on signs and cues.

Have you noticed how life always wins? Regardless of what's coming at you, regardless of how much you resist it, or deny it, or try to control it, it happens. You can't fight fate. Some things are simply meant to happen and they're going to happen and this is what is true. In these times you are brought to your knees in humility. You understand just how little control you truly have, even over your own life. You can plan and steer and direct your world all you want, but in the end, life will come barrelling down and step in.

To resist causes deep stress and imbalance. It causes pain and suffering. Whether an illness or a break up, whether you saw it coming or did not see it coming, whether you 'attracted' it or not... life has intervened. And there is only ever one thing to do. Accept it.

It is your struggle and non-acceptance that causes the most pain, not the event itself. You may be afraid of what's coming, you may be afraid of a new way of living, but are you so sure that the old way was better?

You are conditioned to believe that you can do anything, but this is not quite true. There are limitations. You are not bulletproof, and when something arises or changes you feel frightened, powerless and desperate. This is because you are not a force of nature. Life is.

Become adaptable to change and fluidity because the truth is, this is what life is all about. Remind yourself of this constantly. Be willing to let go of what needs to go, and be willing to accept what needs to come. It's going to anyway, and you can add to your pain with struggle and denial, or allow it to unfold gracefully and then work with it; mould it to work best in your favour.

There is one place in life you are absolutely guaranteed to succeed, where you cannot possibly fail - you cannot possibly fail at being you! Why would you choose to be anyone else? Why would you not proudly show up in the world, loving your appearance, your style, personality, humour, knowledge and talents, all of which are uniquely yours? Why would you not create a life you love and a career that is centred around full alignment with who you are, while being of service and value to the world?

Sure, you can try to look like a second rate version of someone else, or you can pretend to be someone you are not. You can hide your quirks and imperfections and you can show the world your highlight reels, and you will fail at them all. Because you are living an illusion. The illusion that you are trying to live someone else's life. Or rather, the eventual dawning that you have not lived yours.

You cannot fail at being you because you will always attract the right people into your life. You will always encounter only those challenges that help you to become a better and stronger person. Do you see? Everything in your life supports you in being *you*. You may be an artist, a healer, or a scholar. You may be a connector of people, of ideas, or simply enthral the world with your wisdom. Whoever you are, be that person, and you can't possibly fail.

Do not ever dismiss your problems as being insignificant. Yes, there are people whose suffering is in some way harder or worse than yours, but does your life matter any less? Does telling yourself that others have got it worse than you make their problems any better? Has your denial of your own issues helped them solve theirs? You are the only one who decides what 'class' problem you have. You are the only one who decides how big or painful your problem is. You are the only one who gets to choose how to lick your own wounds.

Perhaps you are dealing with a loan that fell through, or missing out on that job. Perhaps your concerns are not around feeding your family or global tragedies. Perhaps you have not yet faced the death of a loved one. But you – your life – is important. You matter. Your feelings matter.

Everyone goes through challenge and difficulty. Do not believe appearances that indicate otherwise. Where there is no challenge, there is no growth.

Are you embarrassed that your problems are 'small' and yet you still complain? Well, do you want bigger ones? We are each receiving the challenges necessary for our individual growth. Our problems provide the lessons we require for this lifetime. For some, these seem relatively 'small'. For others, they can be earth shattering.

But it's not about the size of the problem, it's about the impact. If it hurts, if it affects your life, it matters. So treat your issues with respect and take the time you need to resolve and clear them from your life in a healthy and positive manner.

You won't succeed because you are lucky, or because you are special in any way. You won't succeed because you're good looking or are born for greatness, or because the stars are aligned in your favour. You won't succeed because a psychic told you or because of the Law of Manifestation. You won't succeed because you're well intentioned or have a burning desire.

You will succeed because you did the work. You did what it took. You will succeed because you did the work when you least felt like it. When you were least motivated. When you simply couldn't be bothered. You will succeed because you showed up and did the work regardless. You will succeed because you did what most of the population won't. You did the work when it was hard. When it was inconvenient. And when you fell and all the others gave up, you got back up and kept going. You will succeed because life rewards action. It rewards commitment and the honesty and integrity it takes to see a commitment through to the very end. You will succeed because you know the truth.

You know that if you're not prepared to go all in then you're not truly committed. You know that at this point you need to ask yourself what the price of your dream is. And then decide if you're willing to pay it.

It's easy to do things and it's even easier to not do them. Missing a day here or there doesn't seem all that bad; it doesn't seem to matter, but after a short time you've missed so much that you've formed a pattern of neglect, and some area of your life is about to break down. You may start neglecting your personal daily practise of discipline, which empowers you and sets you up for the day ahead, and after a while you find you're becoming unproductive, unfocused and out of balance.

You may start neglecting your daily practise of exercise and nutritional eating, and one day at a time, one junk meal at a time, one skipped workout at a time, you suddenly find yourself out of shape and not so healthy.

You may start neglecting your attention to your partner, and before you know it, there's a distance, they feel unloved and perhaps they're pulling away.

You may start neglecting your attention to your goals; you've dropped the ball, and now the enthusiasm is waning, the excitement is fading away. You're losing motivation.

Neglect is simple and all it takes is to stop doing things. How easy is that? But neglect is like a poison which can spread throughout your life. It's a killer of all that you've built up and worked so hard to maintain. Neglect is a very easy habit to fall into; it happens quickly, and yet it can take years to reverse the damage.

The simple antidote is small, consistent action, every single day. Neglect anything, but never neglect this.

It's a strange paradox, the concept of presence. No one really has a clue how to do it. You may be at work and yet you're thinking of your problems at home, and when you're at home you're thinking about what needs to be done at work. You say you need more time with the kids, but when you're with your kids, you're on your phone, or busy thinking about other matters that need your attention.

You go through the day constantly pre-occupied with thoughts; thoughts of what could/should have been handled better in the past, or what needs to be done in the future. You listen half-heartedly to others, hearing the words, while your mind is off somewhere else. You are always anywhere but right here. Your whole life is spent in a constant strive for achievement, of planning, of looking forwards, and while these are important, you need to be careful not to miss the point entirely. Life is also about being here, right now.

Learn to be wherever you are, fully. Do whatever you are doing in this moment, fully. Engage with, and listen to that person, fully. Discipline your mind to bring itself back when it starts to wander away. Don't wait until the day you've realised you missed your kid's school concerts, even though you were physically there. Or that you should have told your loved ones more often how much they mattered, while you still had them by your side. Wherever you are, be there.

Take a quick inventory of your life. Not just an inventory of your physical life or your circumstances, but of your feelings and emotions. How do you feel? How do you feel a lot of the time? How are you feeling, right now? How do you feel about your life, or aspects of your life, and how do these feelings show up? Is it stress or anxiety? Is it lethargy, where you just want to sleep and escape the world? Are you suddenly becoming ill, seemingly out of the blue?

Pay close attention to these clues, as your emotions are extremely accurate indicators of your overall well-being. If you are living under circumstances that are painful, difficult or stressful, and you continue to do so - continue to accept them - and not take steps to change them, you will become ill. Emotionally, spiritually, and eventually, physically ill. The mind-body connection is very, very real and this is true. It may be that you find it difficult to change your circumstances. You are urged to find a way. If you cannot remove yourself from the situation, perhaps there is something from the situation that can be removed.

Make every attempt to restore balance to your spirit. What has been taken away from you that you now need to reclaim? What does your soul cry out for? Listen to your first impulse, listen to what you hear repeatedly and then act on this. It is non-negotiable for your spiritual health. You absolutely must.

Never trade your own well-being to keep another happy or comfortable. You are a sovereign being; you retain full power over your health and this can never be compromised.

Sometimes it feels as though the pain will never end. It gnaws relentlessly at your heart. You replay the reel in your minds eye, constantly searching for clues for what went wrong. Yes, it hurts. It can be unbearable. Your life is in chaos; broken and confused. But know this. It will not last. This too, shall pass. You may feel as though you are cracking wide open, and yet these cracks are filling you with light, with love, with new insight and understanding. They are helping you to love yourself and life, bigger and harder than before.

One day this will all be behind you, and you will be moving towards something that you cannot conceive right now. You cannot imagine right now, who or what awaits you in your future. What a wonderful thought to cling to! Do not stop believing that the best is yet to come. It is.

Right now, your wounds are so deep that you cannot imagine that healing will ever take place. Perhaps you do not even know how you will go on. Even so, know that strange and sometimes painful things happen to challenge your growth. It happened because it was no longer challenging your growth. This is the nature of life. You win, you lose, and so the cycle goes.

As you release your pain and heal your wounds, you will slowly begin to unfurl, and you will discover a new love for yourself and for life. This is the new beginning you were waiting for. The new people you need will show up. Synchronicity will present itself in stunning ways.

This is the moment your heart will swell in utter understanding and gratitude for the mysterious ways of the universe.

"When we are no longer able to change a situation, we are challenged to change ourselves." – Viktor Frankl

There will be times when life will deal you a hand and there is absolutely nothing you can do, other than to accept it. It may be incredibly unfair and unjust, or it may just be inconvenient. For certain, it is life changing, and while you are the judge of what the event means for you, the fact is, it's happened and nothing will change it.

Under these circumstances emerges the most painful part of all. You are forced to face-off with yourself. You are asked to delve deeply into your own psyche, into your soul, to discover your strength and your capacity for acceptance, healing and compassion. How often have you been called to do this? How often do you dive beneath the surface of yourself to discover what you are capable of enduring?

And here is where you will be challenged. You will be challenged to change. Your comfort, your certainty, your beliefs, all of these will be ripped away from beneath you in a complete and total upheaval. Your ignorance and innocence will vanish. You will need to draw from the deepest strength you never knew you had.

And you will do this, because you have more strength inside of you than you have ever had to call upon. You have more capacity and tolerance for fear and pain than you ever knew. And, you will do this because there is no other option but to do so.

And when you are caught up in an intolerable situation, know this. You have the power to change everything with one decision. It will require tremendous courage, but that is all it will require. Your willingness to be courageous, just once. You cannot live in soul pain forever, and life won't always rush in to fix things for you. No, life requires that you step up and make the decisions you need to make. It requires you to take responsibility for yourself. It's time to stop hoping for intervention, for magic, for the stars to align, and instead make the changes your life needs. You must do this.

One decision can alter the very fabric of your life. A series of decisions will leave your life so transformed it will be unrecognisable. You know what decisions you need to make. Do not keep waiting for fate to force your hand, for you may not like what fate has in store for you. Stand from a position of power. Be resolute. Even when your chin is quivering, lift your head and focus on what this change will bring you. It will hurt to let go, but it will hurt even more to hold on.

Make your decisions and do not back away. And when your mind begins to flood your senses with all the possible things that may go wrong as a result, tempting you to backpedal – and it will – make the decision to simply pay them no attention. It's just a decision. You can do this.

All of us will face decisions and life changes that are terrifying. All of us, for the most part, will hope that somehow it sorts itself out. But all of us inherently recognise when something is no longer serving us in any way. And in these times when the doubts creep in, drop down into your heart and listen to what lies there.

Find some quiet time, be still and connect with yourself. Ask your soul what it wants. What does it need?

It may come as a sense of knowing, an image or a feeling. You may open to a flood of tears. It may re-connect you with a long forgotten desire. Trust that whatever comes up for you first, is the true and honest response. And then do it today, without delay. Listen to what you are guided to do and do that thing.

The feelings of despondency, of heaviness, is the yearning of your soul. It is what you feel when you are focused on the needs of others above your own. It is the pain of being on the wrong path. Or, when it is simply being ignored. It cries for your attention and in the absence of it, you wonder why you feel so sad, so unfulfilled. So unhappy.

Deep within you is the vessel for your creativity, your purpose and your place on this planet. It is the seat of your joy and inspiration.

This vessel is your soul. Speak to it often.

When your shadow side comes knocking, let it in. You can try to ignore it or outrun it, but at some point you will be triggered to expose it. Eventually you will simply run out of energy to fight it. This is the side of yourself that you fear, that you despise, that you keep hidden away, hoping it will never surface. It's the part of you that you least want to face. And yet this is why it remains your shadow. It is always lurking in the background.

So what is it? It's your response to life when you feel threatened. It's your response when you feel uncomfortable, or when you are in pain. It's your most darkest and most vicious. It's your addiction and dependancy. It's your breaking down and falling apart. It's your inability to cope. It's both your greatest fear and greatest weakness. It is everything you work hard to conceal from the world. Your shadow is you at your most basic and most primal. In a society geared upon appearances and behaviour, this aspect of yourself is neither acceptable nor desirable and you work hard to keep it well hidden.

You pretend it's not there, yet suppression makes it more volatile. Meet it where it is. Know your triggers, and rather than using distraction and avoidance, get to a quiet and safe place and face it. Like an electrical current, just let it run through your system. Do not be afraid: it is only an experience of yourself.

Feel what needs to be felt, and release what needs releasing. Figure out a positive and safe manner in which to interact with yourself. Learn how to talk this aspect of yourself down to a less threatening state. Give it the acknowledgement it's looking for.

Life is ever evolving and so are you. Today you are a different person; a better person than the person you were five years ago. You will even notice you have changed over the last year of your life alone - as it should be. When you change, everything changes along with you. When your thoughts change, your feelings, desires and goals change. Your relationships change too, with people coming into your life and people leaving. Perhaps even your career changes.

Change filters through to every aspect of your life. You cannot change one, or even two areas of your life, and have everything else remain the same. This is because YOU have changed, at your core. You are the common denominator in your life, after all.

But what happens when one day you realise you no longer want the relationship? You may have invested years into it. You may have children. How do you navigate this?

Or you decide you want the job that will require relocation? How will this affect your partner's job? What if one day you simply realise you want far more out of life than you've gotten? What do you do when your soul is crying out?

The easy answer is to follow your heart, but even this is not always practical, and when your decisions affect others, they need to be handled with sensitivity. So this creates a conflict. Do you pursue what may very possibly bring you fulfilment and happiness, or ignore your own needs to keep those around you safe and comfortable?

Search for the most ecological solution. How can the situation best serve everyone involved? And then project yourself out into the future. Which choice you would regret the most?

Is it that you are unhappy with your life? What is it that makes you feel this way? Do you feel stagnant and frustrated? Are all of your dreams 'over there', while you are stuck 'here'? Is this the cause of your unhappiness? That you desperately want the future to come rushing into the present? Perhaps you do not like where you are right now, but right now is exactly where you are. And 'right now' is your only point of power. This is the only place from where you can change anything.

You have fooled yourself into believing you are unhappy. You are not unhappy with your life. You are unhappy with waiting for better. You want all of your tomorrows, today. And very few people can deal with this.

Understand that what you do today, what you think and believe and act on today, will create your tomorrows. You cannot skip the work. It cannot be done for you. And do not wait. Do not wait for a miracle or an intervention. Do not wait for someone to solve your problems, for in doing so they will have acquired further skills for themselves. And what will you have learned? What skills will you have for the future challenges that most certainly await?

Inaction breeds unhappiness. Desperation, too. Do not wait for your moment of desperation to propel you into action for you will make desperate choices.

Take an eagle eye view of your life. See the whole picture. Witness your potential; witness all that you already have, and then make a plan of action. And in the absence of any miracles, begin to love your life. Begin to feel excitement for the journey, for each step you are taking right now is leading you towards the next chapter of your life.

You want to know that everything will be ok, that the decisions you make are the right ones, the person you are with is right for you, that you will continue to enjoy good health and have the things you want in life. But life does not come with assurances and guarantees. There is no such thing as certainty because nothing is certain. Life is ever changing, moving and evolving. Nothing ever stays the same.

You are not powerless in life, but to the extent that you are able to become adaptable and flexible and receptive to change, you will certainly enjoy it more. To the extent that you can see life as something you create for yourself, you will also see that even if your creation were to be swept away, you are able to rebuild from the ground up again. This is true power. It is not in what you own, but rather, knowing that if you lost it all tomorrow, you could build it all again.

You can't control outcomes and you can't control people. The best you can do is to be the kind of person that you, yourself would admire. Forge ahead with a kind heart, good intentions, something wonderful to look forward to, and a joyful willingness to work with what unfolds.

End those relationships whose time has come, get out of that soul-sucking job you hate that gives you zero fulfilment and obligations you just don't want to have, clear the suffocating debt, and change those circumstances you feel powerless to change, because you can.

Get into the mindset of what you can get from life, instead of just getting through it.

If life is a journey and not a destination, then it is equally true that life is less about what you achieve, and more about what you discover along the way. Achievements are the prize, the trophy, the reward for a job well done, and this is important. Life is about enjoyment after all, you can and should strive to do better for yourself and for those around you. It makes you stronger, more confident and more capable.

But life is also about engaging all of your senses, tasting all of its flavours. Throwing yourself wholeheartedly into your passions, travelling the world and experiencing the most beautiful and sacred places, meeting new people and building relationships that will last a lifetime. Finding out what more you can do and how far you can push yourself. Developing a wider perspective, a more open mind and a higher level of compassion and patience. Inspiration won't be found in a 'groundhog day' existence.

Feeling alive is paying attention to what you have a hunger to experience and then drawing this into your reality. It's in challenging yourself, constantly. Placing yourself in the footsteps of others; their cultures, their way of living, and learning that there are other ways to experience life.

It's in being able to savour the waiting, the build-up, the slow anticipation of success. Of simply enjoying the freedom of working towards a goal without necessarily needing the outcome.

It can be very much like planning a holiday. It's that sweet anticipation that gets you excited before you've even departed. That's the journey. That's the real enjoyment.

Stay firmly in your own lane. Keep your focus on your goal. Do not distract yourself by looking over your shoulder at what others are doing. That is their business. Keep your mind firmly on your own. If you're busy minding the business of others, who is minding yours? And, do not halt your progress in comparison. No one is ever going for the same goal, because as unique human beings we can only bring ourselves to the goal and no one else can replicate this. So it's futile to think someone is doing it better. It's such a waste of precious time.

What's another waste of time? Doing something that is not in any way going to contribute to your future or your goals. You will have been involved in relationships, jobs or even circumstances that didn't work out, and you hoped that they would, but for whatever reason they just didn't. This is okay.

It's a part of your wider experience, and it certainly did give you a learning curve.

But to get involved in something which doesn't in any way align with your vision, your goals, or that doesn't have any potential at all to even bring you any relevant or useful experience is simply a massive waste of your time. It's just insanity.

Why would you stay in the relationship that you know is going nowhere? Why would you take a job that has absolutely no stepping stones or connection to your vision? Begin to look at where you may be doing this. Begin to look at what is completely out of place. Where are you wasting time? Where are you not aligning yourself with the vision you have for yourself?

As you journey along your path with learning, growth and new experiences, you will become excited with what you discover. You will be thrilled that you learned 'this' and that you overcame 'that', and sometimes, you will simply become aware of a consciousness that you never had before. You will begin to see life – and your life in particular – in a new light. And you will think this so profound that everybody needs this information. And so you will share it with good intentions; to awaken them, to help them perhaps apply this learning to their own life, and solve a piece of their own puzzle.

You need to know that not everyone is ready. Not everyone is ready for their own truth, let alone yours. Some will not be receptive to your words and they may even tell you that you are being delusional. It may conflict with their thoughts on spirituality and religion, and so for some, your information may even be distressing.

In turn this may distress you. You may feel as though you have overstepped a boundary. Or that you have damaged your relations. Do they think you're weird? Will they now avoid you? It becomes the topic that everyone very carefully and deliberately avoids. But there is no reason for discomfort. It is quite normal and natural for us all to have our own beliefs, because all beliefs are valid. And nor do you need to suppress your voice and your truth. What you simply need to do is find your tribe. Find the people who are where you are, and have these conversations with them.

Everyone finds what they need for themselves in their own time. When they are ready, they will seek answers. Perhaps they will seek them out with you and perhaps they won't, however, they have the right to their truth, and to discover their truth, their way.

A bad day does not make a bad life. You are going to have bad days. You will feel sad, down and defeated. You won't feel like talking and you certainly won't feel like 'showing up'. You may be affected by the cycles of your body, or planetary alignments. You might just be feeling down because you are, and it is this simple.

Perhaps your deepest fears will seem to have caught up with you and the wolves are howling at your door. All of your challenges seem magnified and intensified. Your defences have dropped, your courage is gone and all there are is tears. Life is like this. Everyone goes through periods of darkness. Everybody succumbs to moments of weakness. Everyone at some point, feels like giving up and giving in. And it doesn't have to be about attracting 'bad things' through your 'negative thinking'. Life is life, and things happen. You have struggles, challenges and illness, and this is nothing more than life. There doesn't have to be anything more to it than this.

You also know that these moments will pass. This is the only thing you need to remind yourself. In a day or two, or even a week, you will feel different. Your thoughts and thinking will be in a far better place. Your personal issues, although still present, will seem less threatening, less significant. They will certainly seem more manageable. You will once again feel strong and powerful.

Do not view your entire life through the lens of a temporary slump in motivation and attitude. Do not make decisions while in this state. Go with it, know it will pass, let it pass, and get back up when you are ready.

There is only so much that you can worry about. There is only so much that your body will allow you to feel stress before you begin to see the symptoms on a physical and emotional level. You can run it through your mind over and over, you can twist and turn it around and view it from all angles, but there will come a time - an overwhelming time - when you have absolutely no choice but to just let it go.

You see, life is like a jigsaw puzzle. You cannot force some pieces to fit. And in this moment, while you are trying to force and manipulate something into being, or to bend it in your favour, you will realise that you cannot. In this moment your discomfort will be so acute, you will feel so powerless, and the only thing you can do is let it go. You literally hand it over, all of it, to the ethers. You can hand it over to whomever you feel comfortable handing it to, but you must hand it over. You must trust that there are things in life you cannot handle on your own. Just let it go. How? You just do it. It's an instant decision. You cease struggling and fighting and you gather the courage to let it play out as it will. You simply trust that it will work itself out.

Yes, this takes a lot of faith. It takes enormous courage. And sometimes you simply have no choice. But you will find that with the decision to let go, will come huge relief. You will feel a very tangible shift. You will feel as though your burden has shifted, and along with this, you will feel your faith in life will strengthen. Through the practice of releasing that which you cannot control, you will learn to trust more and more, that life always conspires for your highest good.

What more is life than a series of choices made over time? Every choice you have ever made over your entire lifetime has brought you to this moment in time.

Every choice has led you to your current occupation.

Every choice has led you to your current relationships.

Every choice has led you to your current state of health.

Regardless of whether you love it or not, whether it's what you wanted or not, whether you feel that life is unfair or not, be mindful that you are where you are due to your choices. This is not about 'blame'. It is a truth for us all. Whether the choices were conscious and deliberate, and made with intention to move you towards your desired goals, or whether they were made without conscious intent, or out of fear, with no thoughts for future consequences, it is all the same.

You make a decision; it leads you towards a certain outcome. Can you see the enormous power you hold? You can make any decision at any point in time, and shift your entire destiny, forever. And do not think it is too late to change that which makes you unhappy. Do not settle for mediocrity because you can't be bothered starting over, or because you think it will take too long. The time will pass anyway. And you have absolutely no idea what life has planned for you, or how long it will take.

Your future may come rushing in to you all at once. Your decision to make a change may have been the sign that life was waiting for.

How do you know you are choosing from love versus fear? How do you know you are in alignment with yourself and your purpose? Because your choices feel right. Whatever you do, works. The steps you are taking are moving you towards a goal; towards a desired outcome. You feel positive and proactive, even in the face of challenging circumstances. You keep going because something within is driving you to keep going. Everything is lining up – your intentions, your visions and your actions.

You get excited about life and you desire to be of service, in whatever forms of expression your talents take. You make your decisions from a place of power and confidence and your life takes on an easy flow. It's not that you no longer face difficulties, it's that you know how to overcome them. You find solutions and you just keep going.

Fear is quite the opposite. You make decisions from desperation, and they are made from a need to move away from something, such as getting out of a job or leaving a relationship, so it's about escaping. You react, rather than take focused action, and in this state of mind, you are likely to choose 'anything', even if it isn't in your best interests.

Fear doesn't feel so good. In fear, you feel stressed, worried, nervous and anxious. Things feel hard. You might think you are doing all the 'right things' but keep coming up against barrier after barrier. You are not in alignment, you are not living your truth, and therefore, you are trying to force into being that which is not for you.

Create a plan for yourself that feels good and right, and takes you into the direction of your dreams. Listen carefully to your instincts and intuition and notice whenever your path seems blocked. Use your guidance system, learn to work with it. Develop the acuity to sense when it's time to change your approach and when you are simply going off in the wrong direction.

When did you become so convinced that life was entirely the result of your negative thoughts? When did you decide it seemed quite normal to 'blame' yourself for the bad things in your life? Sure, it's a universal truth that you need to take responsibility for your choices, decisions and actions. It's just a very decent, human thing to do. But is it entirely true that you are the cause of everything?

Do not accept so much responsibility that you are letting others off the hook. Everyone is responsible for what they bring to the table. What if life is simply happening? Can you really manifest ill health? Bad things do happen to good people. You can eat well, exercise, take your vitamins and do 'all the right things' and you can still develop illness, even serious ones. You can and should most certainly do your best to maintain excellence in your health, but do not ever believe that nursing a heartache or feeling sad will manifest an illness. Is it not okay to get angry with life? Of course it is. But you won't create illness because of that.

People do part ways and not because one or the other did anything 'wrong', but because they simply grew apart. Did they necessarily manifest it, or were two people simply wrong for each other? Life happens.

By all means, be positive in your thoughts. If for no other reason than it just feels better than being down and pessimistic. But there is no need to micro-manage your thoughts to the point of exhaustion. Not everything has a neat and tidy explanation. Things will go wrong and this is just life.

At times, life can certainly deal you a difficult hand. You feel broken. Your spirit is broken. It's not that you can't go on, you feel that you don't want to. You wonder what you did to deserve 'this'. You're not alone. Life can be tough and unfair and you can't 'positive think' your way through everything. Nor should you try. True freedom and healing comes from facing the truth of your life as it is, not as it 'could' be if only you adjusted your thinking. Do not pretend you are not in pain. Do not pretend that your life has not frozen over. Because here's what is true.

You need to give your feelings the time and respect they deserve. Patients with broken bones are not encouraged to jump back into activity in order to heal faster, so why is a broken heart or a broken spirit any different? We are aware that in time, the hurt will mend. We also know that as the mending begins, we can slowly begin to re-integrate back into our usual activities, and in most cases, we discover new interests to pursue. Thus we can see the event as moving us along into a new direction.

You know you will fly again. Inside of you, you know this. And you will do so with more life experience, and greater strength and appreciation for yourself and what you are capable of overcoming and achieving. Do what you need to do, to heal. And remember that soon enough, you will once again find joy, love and laughter in your life.

From little things, come big things, and this is true. When you learn to become an excellent custodian of anything – money, time, love or relationships – in smaller increments, you will find you are soon entrusted with their safekeeping in larger proportions.

How much money you will accumulate – and hold onto – is in direct proportion to how well you manage the small amount you have now. Do you tend to spend frivolously? Or not at all, because of a scarcity mindset that money is hard to come by? Neither of these attitudes will particularly serve you well, but it is all about your habits and mindset. Regardless of whether it's one thousand dollars or one million dollars, you will manage your money in the same way.

The richness and quality of your relationships is in direct proportion to your capacity to nurture and contribute to each individual. Love, care and respect will help your interactions develop to a more meaningful level. A selfish approach will drain everybody's energetic resources, and you will wake up one day and realise you have no meaningful relationships at all.

Life will always give back in direct proportion to what you put in. It cannot be any other way. What you plant, feed and nurture will flourish and bring you untold joy. What is neglected and abused will always wither away and die.

Because you have so much goodness and kindness, you will naturally go out of your way to help others. As a caring human being, you will seek out solutions to help and guide others in their times of need. And where there are no solutions to be found, you will stand by their side in friendship, support and respect. Being of service to those around you, and the world, is an act of profound kindness and love. You will never fully understand just how much of a difference you have made to someone else's life.

However, there are some people who simply do not want your help, and nor do they want to help themselves. Perhaps you've met these people? The ones to whom you have given your time and energy, advice and experience, over and over, and yet months or even years later, they remain the same. Absolutely nothing ever changes. They still have the same issues, challenges and complaints. Do not give away your power and energy in this way. Your energy is your life force, and this is precious.

You will be left drained, frustrated and feeling somehow responsible. You are not. Do not become convinced it is your work to save people. Like you, they have their path to walk, and like you, their lessons to learn. Sometimes in your efforts to help others, you will rob them of a most precious gift; the gift of discovering their own power. Of learning to cope with life. Allow them this. Allow them their mistakes and the satisfaction of overcoming their challenges, themselves.

Do not apologise for your existence. Do not make yourself small, or diminish yourself in any way. Never feel that you 'owe' anything to anyone. You do not. Do not stay quiet to keep others comfortable, or apologise for being you, and make yourself less visible. Do not be afraid of speaking your mind and voicing your desires.

You will threaten the security of those around you, of this be certain. You will threaten their sense of power and control, for what influence do they have when you are fully on your feet? And they may tell you they supported you, supplied for you. And this may be true. They may make you feel guilty for spreading your wings and wanting to fly, but know this:
You owe them nothing.

You supplied and supported for them, too. You gave to them in a clear exchange - a mental, emotional, spiritual and physical exchange - and it was an equal exchange, for did they not stick around? They may try to convince you that you cannot succeed, and most certainly without them, but see beyond this illusion. They are scared. They are scared of being left behind.

It is time to spread your wings! It's time to be bold, to move on with your life, and to do so unapologetically. It's time to claim your joy and happiness *right now*, for if not now, then when?

The story belongs to the storyteller. And the storyteller, dear friend, is you. What are your stories? What stories have defined your life? What do you tell yourself time and time again about why you are where you are? Or the stories of what happened to you along the way that prevent you from being positive about the future? What stories get in the way of pursuing your dreams? What stories of yours prevent you from experiencing meaningful relationships and life experiences?

And about those stories. Do you ever wonder why you continue to tell them? Do they keep you protected? Do you gain sympathy? Ask yourself why you need this. Why do you need to remain helpless and powerless? Yes, perhaps your stories are real, and perhaps they are very painful. Perhaps also, it is time to move on from this. You do not have an infinite supply of time. At what age will you decide to be free? At what age will you allow yourself to enjoy your life to the fullest? Write another story.

One where you are the hero of your own journey. Where you are strong, focused, motivated and powerful. Where you have overcome the greatest trials, and will do so again and again because you have the skills to do so. A story where you are the leader; inspiring, courageous and a beacon of light to others.

Why would you not? Why would you not choose to claim the very best for yourself? Why would you not leave behind those who seek to hold you back and imprison you in the story of their own misery? You have hurt enough. It is time to fly.

Strip back your life and simplify. Remove that which clutters your mind, your soul and your life. A huge task, but well worth your peace of mind and lightness of being. Begin right now. What is it that causes you stress? What situations or people are taking up space in your thoughts, that you simply don't need to be thinking or worrying about? Let them go. Now. In this moment.

What has to come to an end? What relationships are doing more harm than good? What behaviours are you tolerating that have now become intolerable? Do something about these now. What is intruding on your personal space and freedom? Who or what seems to be holding you back? Now is the time to stand up. Now is the time to ask them to step away.

What thoughts have become habits? What are you thinking that is causing you to lose confidence and belief in yourself?

Replace them now. Fill your mind with powerful thoughts about who you are and what you stand for.

Look around your personal space, your home. Does this really reflect who you are, or who you've become? Clear it all out and be brutal. Clear your space to clear your energy. When was the last time you re-arranged the furniture to freshen it up? Do that now.

Stop allowing others to dictate your terms and conditions. Stop backing down and backing away. Stand up for your life! Stand up for your right to joy and success and fulfillment. To living your life, your way, on YOUR terms.

Difficult times can trigger some aspects of trauma and stress. Sometimes even shock. What happens when someone you know sinks deeply into a depressed state and refuses all offers of help? It may be helpful to understand that they are feeling vague and confused, and in this state even they do not know what help they need. So go easy. Go slow.

You may be tempted to rush in and help and they may withdraw and refuse your offers. Understand this. More than likely you have also experienced such times in your own life so you know that sometimes there is no easy fix. Sometimes words are not adequate. Sometimes you don't actually want anyone to help make things better, because the truth is, you're still processing the event and you simply need time for yourself.

Do not be offended. Let them hate life. Let them get angry. Let them cope as best as they can. Learn to notice when to let them be. When to give them space. But don't give up on them; flicker quietly in the background.

You can help in silent ways. Help them with the small things that may slip their mind; cook them some meals or clean up their place. Do their shopping or gardening. Write them a note and buy some flowers. You can be of greater assistance simply by taking over the tasks that would free up their time to focus on healing.

You have the right to pursue love, for love's sake. You have the right to desire passion, to desire company, to desire the beautiful sensation of being wrapped up in a warm embrace. To be loved. You have the right to pursue the one night only. You have the right to enjoy the act of sex without attachment. Your needs are sacred and should be honoured.

Do not allow others to reduce your heart's desires to insignificance. They will tell you that you are whole and complete as you are, on your own. They will tell you that your focus should be on your own self-love. They will tell you that you don't actually need anyone else. And you know they are right. You know that the most powerful love affair of your life will be with yourself, so love who you are, and also love who you are not. Love yourself because it simply feels better than the opposite. And because you are a powerful expression of all that is good and pure.

But life is nicer when it's shared. Life feels better with human touch. You feel lonely and crave someone to hold. You desire intimacy. You want to feel love and adoration from another human being. There is nothing wrong with this.

You often wear a mask, a tough exterior that tells the world you're strong and powerful and fine on your own. You do this because to do otherwise is seen as a weakness and 'needy'. It's vulnerable. And sometimes, you are shamed for your needs and desires. You have the right to want someone in your life, to love, and be fully loved. You do not need to justify nor explain this to anyone. Do not feel bad or desperate. Follow your heart and be open to what unfolds for you.

Every day is a brand new day. A brand new set of choices and decisions. A brand new set of opportunities. A brand new perspective. Every day is a new chance to do things differently.

If yesterday you were hiding in fear, today make the choice to be brave.

If yesterday you were feeling despondent and negative, today choose to be positive and excited.

If yesterday you acted outside of your values, today begin to act with integrity.

If yesterday you couldn't be bothered, today drop the excuses and take action.

If yesterday you felt hopeless and confsed, today create a clear and powerful vision for your life.

If yesterday you were angry and hateful, today be filled with love and gratitude.

If yesterday you wanted to give in, today you can gather your strength and lift your attitude.

If yesterday a goal fell through, today you can try again, with a different approach.

If yesterday you hurt someone, today you can make things right.

Today you can do everything different. You can make new choices and better decisions. You cannot change your yesterdays, but you certainly can and will influence all of your tomorrows. You have so much more within you than a lazy attitude and negativity. Don't lose heart and never lose hope; if yesterday knocked you over, today you must get back up and keep going.

Pain is necessary for the breakthrough. Life will always reach a maximum point of discomfort at any time you are about to jump to a higher level of consciousness. Your breakthrough will force you to push past your limits. These will feel both frightening and sickening, but on the other side of this you will feel more alive than you ever have before. You will not escape these phases, and phases are all they are. They are painful and intense. They will consume your mind, your energy and your life, but they will pass. And what is this breakthrough?

It is a moment of profound realisation or change. It is the moment you are pushed over the cliff, with or without a safety net. It is the thing that changes your life forever. At first it will be difficult to navigate. At first, there will be fear and pain as you integrate these changes. There may be years of hurt to be healed, or beliefs that have been altered. There may be people you need to release. Or, there may be harsh truths about yourself you need to face. It is profound. And it will heal you.

You will feel, for a while, unfamiliar to yourself. You may feel ungrounded. You will experience many occasions of self-doubt and lack of motivation. You will question the meaning of your life over and over again. Until it all comes together in sudden clarity. You realise what it was all really about. It was about preparation for meeting the future you. The 'you' who is more advanced and better equipped to deal with life. The 'you' who is stronger, more powerful and more assertive. The pain of the breakthough was necessary for you to step into this higher version of yourself.

And you will continue this journey of intermittent breakthroughs because this is the process of life. Always reaching for the next level of your greatest potential.

You have many dreams within you. You have secret fantasies that you dare not utter aloud, and in the safety of quiet moments of solitude you allow yourself to drift away into another world. In this world you are free to be who you want to be. You act out who you deeply desire to be.

These dreams and desires may be about your ideal romance. They may be about a career that passed you by. Or perhaps this is an escape from a life you can barely tolerate. It's good to have somewhere safe to escape. It's good to be somewhere that takes the pressure off, even for a short time. It lets you recalibrate, and gives you something to hold onto.

And perhaps in your real life you do not believe it is possible for your fantasy to become a reality. You think you are too old, too much time has passed or there's not the money to make it happen. Or maybe you 'locked' into circumstances that cannot be changed.

But people do not change because their lives are great. They change because their lives are intolerable. But perhaps your dreams have nothing to do with fame, fortune and success. Perhaps you simply dream of a better life, of freedom, of independence, of choice. Well …why is this not a possible reality for you? Why not you? When you have the mental construct, the vision of what you secretly want for yourself, half the work is done. The rest becomes simple. It's just a matter of following a sequence of steps.

Why not begin with just one? Why not turn just one fantasy into your reality?

You say you've lost confidence in yourself and yet the only way to get confidence is by doing the 'thing' required. You witness yourself standing tall, taking ownership of your life. And then you take on the next challenge. And you become even more confident. And so it goes.

This is the fresh start you've been waiting for. This is your turning point. And it's been in you, all this time. You are, right now (and always have been), only one decision away from changing your entire life. You certainly don't have to; this choice is yours. But do not pretend that you cannot.

You can choose to walk away

You can choose self-respect

You can choose to stop avoiding

You can choose love

You can choose forgiveness

You can choose a new direction

You can choose your thoughts

You can choose to be responsible

You can choose to become healthy and strong

You can choose to be kinder

You can choose to contribute

You can choose to drop judgement

You can choose to be understanding

You can choose to speak up

You can choose to create firm boundaries

You can choose to prioritise yourself

You can choose to educate yourself

You can choose mastery

The truth is, you have the opportunity to create your life any way you wish. If you choose to believe life is nothing but a struggle, you will always experience struggle. If you choose to believe you are 'stuck' you will remain so. If you believe you will remain alone, you will. Is money hard to make? How do you think that one will go for you?

The point is that life will be anything you believe it to be. You are in charge of your experience. Choose a different one.

For what do you feel shame? For what do you shrink and cringe and despise yourself? In what way are you 'wrong?'. Let's flip this around. Life is not much more than a string of experiences. If you can understand that all you are ever doing as you move through time is gathering human experiences, you will cease to feel shame. And these may be pleasant or unpleasant. Preferably they will be both.

From these experiences you will get to choose. Were they good for you or not? Did you enjoy them or not? Are you likely to repeat them or not? You may not be particularly proud of them, they may not have been your finest moment, but they are nothing more than a moment from which you acted with the knowledge you had at the time.

It's easy to judge yourself in retrospect. But the truth is, if you had known better, you would have done better. Shame is an emotion you reach for when you feel something you said or did was wrong. But wrong according to whose moral standards? If a friend reached out to you with the same issue, would you feel they should be ashamed? More than likely you would feel horrified at their level of self-loathing.

Your desires are not shameful. They are experiences you wish to have. And the shame you carry for the actions of another? Never, ever carry the burden of responsibility for another human being. They are fully accountable for their actions, they sought out the experience, and unfortunately perhaps, you were caught up amongst it all. All of us become a part of someone else's story. All of us are a character actor in someone else's play. This is at times unfortunate, but this is the nature of life. Always a new lesson to learn.

For how long will you keep repeating the story, replaying the movie and feeling self-disgust? You had an experience, now release it and find some peace.

Perhaps you grew up in a family of abuse or dysfunction. Perhaps you were neglected and mistreated. You may have been physically harmed. Perhaps even now, today, your family remains the same. Still angry and abusive. And because you don't want this in your life, and you choose to raise your own children differently, you distance yourself, choosing to pretend they don't exist. You may have even cut them out of your life completely.

It hurts. You still carry the scars and the pain. You feel robbed of a proper childhood, one filled with love and affection and encouragement. There is no justification for what you endured. There is no excuse for their behaviour. But please know this, not for their sake, but yours. They were hurting too.

Whoever hurt you so deeply, so terribly, was hurting too. Because no healthy, well rounded, normal human being goes out of their way to hurt another. This is the behaviour of one who is filled with rage, self-loathing, pain and fear.

You were not unloved. You were not unwanted. Somewhere along the way and for whatever reason, something hurt them deeply. Enough to influence how they treated you. And this is unfortunate. Because you see, you cannot give to another that which you don't know yourself.

You are not being asked to forgive, you are being asked to understand that none of what occurred was ever your fault. You were not a bad child deserving of punishment.

But you were taught some valuable lessons, and it did shape you into the person you are today. It did offer you true compassion for others. It did make you love your own family even more. You hold all the power now, you see. Finally, with you, this terrible cycle has been broken.

Any moment in time will only ever come to you once. This moment, right now, is gone forever. Consider this deeply. You will only ever get one shot at any moment – ever. Just drop the pretences. Drop the shyness, the coyness, the 'not knowing', the fear of what 'they' will think, the fear of failure, the fear of success, the fear of being too this or too that.

Right now is all you ever have. You will never come back for a second chance. Start living. Eat the cake, dance naked under the stars, take a younger lover. Do everything that thrills and excites you. Forget about social conditioning, your goal is joy, so go ahead and enjoy yourself, unapologetically. Now is the moment. Not next week or next year.

Stop being so restrictive on yourself and lighten up. Stop depriving yourself. Stop worrying about how you will be judged. If you knew how little your actions actually mattered to others, you would dive head first into life. So dive.

Do not allow people to abuse or mistreat you. Do not. If you wrote a letter to your younger self, what would you say? Take your own advice now, and do not waste a single moment. You are never too old or too sick or whatever excuse you come up with. If you knew how quickly time is passing, how fleeting life is, you would say yes to everything your heart desires.

Get out of your head and into life. Be the person who has stories to tell about all the ridiculous, crazy things they did, instead of crying in regret over a lifetime wasted.

Just for today, lay aside your burdens and rest. Whatever it is that worries or follows you with pain or a heavy heart, just breathe and let it go. Release it all.

How do you do this? You just decide. Decide that for ONE day your physical and emotional state matters more. Just for one day, everything can wait. You can do this. It's just one day. It is not your job to carry the burden alone. It is not your job to solve every problem on your own – indeed, it is arrogant of you to think that it is, or that you can.

You do not need to know where or to whom you release your worries. Your job is to decide that you no longer wish to carry the weight of this responsibility, and to hand it over to powers greater than your own. Your issues will be just fine without you. They may even still be around tomorrow. Allow yourself, for just one day, to not care.

www.ingramcontent.com/pod-product-compliance
Lightning Source LLC
Chambersburg PA
CBHW070614300426
44113CB00010B/1525